SHOWTIME!

over 75 ways to put on a show

Reg Bolton

DK PUBLISHING, INC.

CONTENTS

T 2410

REG BOLTON has been involved in theater since his school days. He has performed and taught many performance arts including magic, mime, street theater, puppetry, juggling, clowning, circus, and film. In 1987, he set a new world record, running the marathon in 3 hours, 45 minutes, and 50 seconds while juggling three balls. Reg holds theater and circus workshops for children, where he passes on his enthusiasm and love of the performing arts. His work has taken him all over the world, including Britain, Norway, Italy, Israel, Japan, China, and the US. Reg now lives with his family in Australia, where he puts on shows with children in many locations, from inner-city schools to remote communities in the Central Desert. In 1996 Reg set up the Circus School in Perth, Western Australia.

A DK PUBLISHING BOOK

Editor Sheila Hanly
US Editor Constance M. Robinson
Art Editor Helen Melville
Managing Art Editor Rachael Foster
Photography Andy Crawford

First American Edition, 1998
2 4 6 8 10 9 7 5 3 1
Published in the United States by DK Publishing, Inc.
95 Madison Avenue, New York, New York 10016

Visit us on the World Wide Web at http://www.dk.com

Library of Congress Cataloging-in-Publication Data
Bolton, Reg.
Showtime!: Over 75 ways to put on a show / by Reg Bolton. -- 1st American ed.
p. cm.
Includes index.
Summary: An activity book with suggestions for simple shows and performances that can be put on alone or as a group. Includes such theatrical activities as ventriloquism, mime, and the production of a full-length play.
ISBN 0-7894-3433-4
1. Children's plays--Presentation, etc.--Juvenile literature.
[1. Theater--Production and direction.] I. Title.
PN3157.B65 1998
792'.0226--dc21   98-22801
                                CIP
                                AC

Color reproduction by Colourscan, Singapore
Printed and bound in Italy by A. Mondadori Editore, Verona

INTRODUCTION

WELCOME TO THE WORLD of show business! This book is jam-packed with ways you can entertain your family and friends. We all have our heroes of stage and screen. They may seem larger than life or superhuman, but they were children once. They were probably nervous at their first performance, but they made it … and so can you. This book will give you the confidence to perform well in public. You can perform alone or with a partner. You may decide to form a company with your friends or help to organize a big school show.

You can put on a show at home, in your backyard, in the park, in a hall, a shopping mall, or at church. You may even produce a special show for a senior citizens' center or a hospital. Whatever you do, have confidence in yourself, be considerate to your partners, rehearse the show well, and give the audience a real treat. Most of all, have fun!

If you have ever been backstage at a theater or in a television studio, you will know how complicated show business can be. So many people! So much equipment! So many strange words! But you don't need all this. This book will show you how you can be a star and have the audience screaming for more — with just a few friends, a little preparation, and a lot of imagination.

REHEARSALS

Some school plays have to be rehearsed for weeks and weeks. Your show can happen much more quickly. As long as you concentrate on your job and give your partners and friends a lot of support, it will all come together. Theaters and film sets are very friendly places where each person does his or her job as well as possible, from actors and stage crew to the person making the sandwiches. How many rehearsals should you have? As many as you need. How long will each rehearsal take? As long as you've got, plus five minutes. And remember the show business motto: *"It will be all right on the night."*

CONFIDENCE

Believe in yourself. Some of the world's greatest performers still get stage fright, but there are ways to deal with it. One way to build your own confidence is to change the way you think and speak. All the time you are planning, preparing, and rehearsing, agree to BAN the words "no," "can't," "impossible," "embarrassing," and "difficult." Once you can perform your own shows with confidence and pride, you will begin to succeed in lots of ways — in school, with friendships, with your whole life!

Reg Bolton

★ BRIGHT IDEAS

Look for stars, such as the one above, throughout the book. You will find one wherever there is a really great show idea.

HELP!

You may need adult help for some of the activities in this book, such as operating stage lights or getting permission to perform in a public place. You should also get adult approval for any show that is especially noisy or that uses lots of borrowed clothes or furniture.

Warning!
You may want to use face paints to perform some of the shows in this book. Always use good-quality paints, and before applying something to your face, test it on a small patch of skin to make sure you are not allergic to it.

HAND PUPPETS

H AND PUPPETS ARE EASY TO MAKE and operate. They may not be action heroes, but at least they can tell good jokes, they sing well, and they can talk with the audience. Here are some simple puppets to make, and great show ideas to try.

Hand Puppet Hints

The Golden Rule of hand puppets: The one who is speaking should be the one who is moving.
Project your voice "through" the puppets by hanging a black curtain in front of your face. You can see the audience, but they can't see you!

Sew loops of wool onto each finger to make hair.

Cut out shapes twice as wide as your fingers, and glue or sew the edges together.

★ GLOVE PUPPETS

You can make puppets with real gloves. Use a ping-pong ball as a head, tuck two fingers inside the glove, as shown, then dress it up. Or draw faces on each finger to make a whole family of characters. If you cut off one glove finger and leave your finger bare, you can perform *The Emperor's New Clothes!*

★ FINGER PUPPETS

You can make lots of different characters in felt using your own designs. You will need some scraps of felt, a pair of scissors, and glue. With these puppets, you can do a really big show with up to ten characters.

★ SOCK PUPPETS

Sock puppets can be very expressive. All you need are three buttons for the eyes and nose, a sock, and lots of expressions. Try these faces.

Happy

With a finger, make a little tuck in the sock so your puppet can smile.

Confused

★ PUPPET THEATER SHOW

Performing in a puppet theater means the audience cannot see you, so your puppets will seem more real. You can also add scenery and props to your show. Why not perform a sing-along musical story, with the puppets conducting the audience and offering candy to the singers?

Chair theater

A chair theater is one of the easiest to set up. You will need two upright chairs with backs of the same height, a broom, four large bath towels, and some safety pins.

Place the chairs facing each other and drape towels over the backs.

Drape a third towel over the chair seats, and a fourth over a broom balanced across the chair backs.

Use safety pins to keep the towels in place.

Cut scenery from pieces of colored cardboard and pin or tape them to the front.

Slip your hand between the back towel and the chair to operate your puppet.

Paint scenery on sheets of paper and tape them inside the box, opposite the stage.

Decorate the front and sides of your theater with bold designs.

Choose a sturdy box that won't wobble or fall over.

Cut along three sides of a large rectangle to make a door.

Big box theater

If you can get hold of a large cardboard box, you can make a full-size puppet theater. Ask an adult to help you cut a hole in the front for a stage, and a door at the back so you can climb inside. Stick hooks at waist height inside the front of the box, so you can hang your puppets upside down for quick changes.

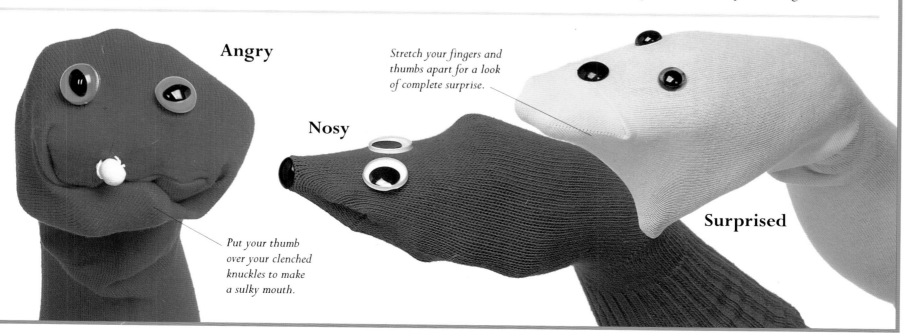

Angry

Nosy

Surprised

Stretch your fingers and thumbs apart for a look of complete surprise.

Put your thumb over your clenched knuckles to make a sulky mouth.

MARIONETTES

S TRING PUPPETS, OR MARIONETTES, can be the most lifelike puppets of all. Professional puppeteers train for years to handle the very complicated controls. But you have to start somewhere, and here are some ideas for performing with simple marionettes you can make or buy.

Loop the handling string around your thumb and little finger. This will give you great control over the snake's movements.

Marionette Hints

You should avoid tangling the strings. To store your marionette, twist the strings together so the controls can't fall between the strings.
If your strings get hopelessly tangled, undo or cut them and start again.
Warm up your hands before a show. Stretch and squeeze them and exercise your fingers one at a time.

Move your hands in a flowing motion. Your snake will do the same, and can glide over your foot.

String a wooden bead between each spool. This gives the snake its slithery, twisting movement.

★ SPOOL SNAKE

This is one of the easiest marionettes to make – simply run a cord through decorated spools and attach handling strings as shown. Get a friend to be a snake charmer and play a recorder or flute, while you make the snake come out of a basket.

★ TWO-STRING PUPPET

These simple puppets have one main string to hold the body, and another attached to the head. The legs hang loose. You can make this ostrich and other exotic beasts, and present a nature documentary, such as "Life in the African Bush."

Make the ostrich change direction by almost lifting the feet off the ground, and swinging the head around.

1 Push a ping-pong ball into the toe of a stocking. Use string to tie it into place. Tie another piece of string 4 in (10 cm) further down the leg.

2 Take a clean, round plastic container, and push it into the leg until it reaches the second knot. Knot the end of the leg behind the tub.

3 Take two pieces of soft cord and tie heavy nuts to them. These are the ostrich's legs. Now tape or sew the cords onto either side of the bottom of the tub.

4 Cut out wings, feathers, and a beak from colored cardboard, and stick them onto your bird. Then attach strings to the head and body as shown on the left.

★ FIVE-STRING PUPPET

With five strings your puppet can do more complicated movements. It can walk, bow, wave, and kick. If you are doing a solo show, you supply the voice as the marionette talks to the audience. How about telling a ghost story?

Use your fingers to lift each string as you need it.

The five strings are attached to the two ends, the two bends, and the top of the coathanger.

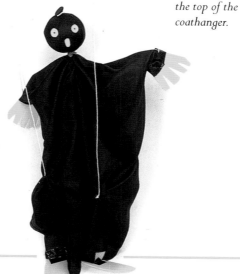

When your puppet lifts its leg or waves, you must hold the control level so the puppet does not rise or fall.

Making hand controls

Squeeze a wire coathanger, and bend both arms forward. Attach five strings with masking tape, then fix the strings to the head, arms, and legs of a jointed rag doll or a puppet made from a big scarf.

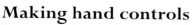

The U-shaped wire is called the control.

★ DANCING PUPPET SHOW

A great show for a marionette is dancing to music. You can act with your puppet when it falls asleep or behaves badly, and you have to persuade it to get on with the show.

Dress all in black, so the audience focuses their attention on the marionette and it can be seen easily.

If you are performing for small children, get them to sit on the floor so the marionette is at eye level.

★ MARIONETTE THEATER SHOW

This marionette theater was made from a large cardboard box, with a space cut for a stage, and other decorations glued or painted onto it. You can also make stage furniture and scenery. This sort of theater is ideal for performing a puppet play – telling a complete story with different characters.

If you don't want the audience to see you, you can extend the theater upward to hide your face.

The marionette theater helps to make the characters seem life-size, and easier to watch (like a television screen).

This play was based on a folktale. Fairy tales are another good source of ideas for plays.

SHADOW THEATER

SHADOW THEATER HAS A GREAT ATMOSPHERE, since the audience is sitting in the dark. Puppets as simple as cardboard cutouts, or even your bare hands, can create wonderful effects. How else could you perform open-tummy surgery in front of an audience?

★ HAND SHADOWS ON A WALL

A hand shadow show is the simplest of all. Tell a story to go with the shapes, and make noises to go with the characters.

Swan
Bend your wrist, so that the swan's neck curves as it glides along. Move your forefinger and thumb to make the swan open and shut its bill.

Dog
If this dog hears a strange noise, it can prick up or wriggle its ears (move your thumbs) and open its mouth to bark or bite (move your little finger).

Bird
Hold your fingers together and move them up and down to flap the wings. Wriggle your thumb tips so the bird can chirp a song.

Old man
This old man can move his mouth to talk (move the middle fingers of your lower hand). If he tells a lie his nose grows (move your lower index finger)!

Rabbit
The little rabbit can twitch its ears and bound along on its large hind legs. It can also pick up things with its front paws (your two fingers).

★ SHADOW BOX SHOW

A good theme for a shadow show is a fairy tale or legend. Each puppeteer can make and operate his or her own creation, and you can be really imaginative with lots of moving parts, including pieces that come apart. The scenery, and even the puppets, can have very detailed shadows made with lacy material, wire, or wool attached to the cardboard. You could also use store-bought toys with clear silhouettes, such as dolls or model cars.

Cut out puppets with bold outlines.

Cut out the eyes.

Use doweling about 12 in (30 cm) long and ⅜ in (1 cm) in diameter, glued or tacked to the back of each moving part.

Use round-head fasteners to hinge just one leg for walking.

Using a thumbtack instead of glue makes it easier to remove the rod to store the puppet between shows.

Make sure you keep your body out of the beam cast by the light behind the theater.

To make this theater, cut a large hole in a shallow box. Tape tracing paper over the hole to make a screen.

★DOOR THEATER SHOW

Choose a door that can be fully opened, then stretch a white sheet across the door and ask an adult to attach it. If you can't attach the sheet to the door, ask some friends to hold a sheet stretched in front of you. This is more difficult because the sheet must be kept tight. You must then place a light behind you and your puppets.

Hold each object away from any other shadows so the audience can see it clearly.

Stand close to the sheet, but do not touch it — this will spoil the effect.

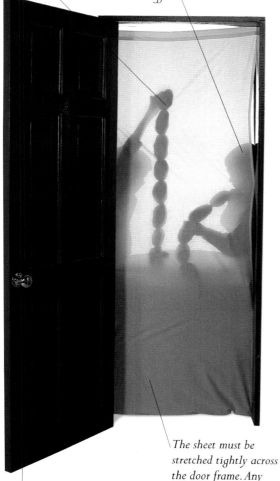

Make sure the door stays open — don't let a sudden gust of wind end your show.

The sheet must be stretched tightly across the door frame. Any wrinkles will distort the shadows.

The operation

You will need two friends to help you act out the following scene. A doctor enters and asks for an assortment of terrifying tools (cardboard cutouts). A nurse brings in the patient, who is put to sleep with a huge hammer. In shadow theater, the hammer does not have to hit the head at all — as long as the shadows touch. Be imaginative with sound effects — for example, a loud bang, then birds tweeting.

Doc: Who is today's victim, er, I mean patient? Nurse: Mrs. Jones... again!

Mrs. Jones: I hope this operation works better than the last one!

Doc: Don't worry, Mrs. Jones. You won't feel a thing.

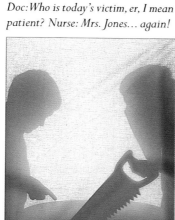

Nurse: I think that's the right spot. Doc: Right, let's open her up.

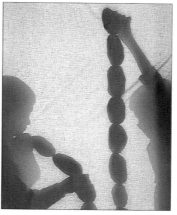

Doc: Keep pulling, Nurse. I've never seen such long intestines.

Doc: Put that bone back — she may need it for walking.

Doc: So THAT's where I left my scissors last week.

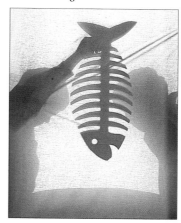

Nurse: Well, now we know what she had for lunch.

Doc: Time for the heart transplant. New heart, please, Nurse.

Doc: Good, we've finished. Now let's sew her up again.

Mrs Jones: Oh, dear. My tummy feels a little SAW!

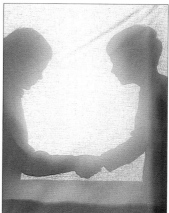

Nurse: Uh-oh. The saw! Well, at least we've got the scissors back.

11

VENTRILOQUISM

AS A VENTRILOQUIST, YOU APPEAR TO HAVE a conversation with a dummy, but really, it is YOU who does all the talking. The key to being a good ventriloquist is not in "throwing" your voice, but in giving your dummy a completely separate personality.

A teddy bear on your lap can look up at you as you tell the story, try to hide during the scary parts, and cry when the story gets sad.

★ THE SIMPLEST DUMMY OF ALL

Draw a face on your hand using face paints or makeup. Then you could wrap your hand in a head scarf, and stick on hair or a beard. Move your thumb up and down to make the dummy speak. This can be very funny if you are entertaining a small number of children.

★ STORYTELLING

Learning to tell a story well can be the first step in becoming a ventriloquist. As you tell a story, change your voice and face for different characters. When a small character speaks, your voice should be light and sweet, with your face looking upward. A giant would reply in a big, gruff voice, looking downward with eyes wide open.

★ A CONVINCING ACT

To be believable, you need to make the two voices different. When it is YOU, speak in your own voice, with lots of mouth movements. When it is your DUMMY, put on a different accent, and keep the dummy MOVING and looking at you or the audience. Keep your own mouth fixed in a half-smile, while your eyes and head movements react to what the dummy says.

"Say 'Good morning, girls and boys!'"

"I can't see any kids."

"Look again. There's an audience out there."

"An audience? You're kidding!"

Ventriloquism Hints

Try to say "ventriloquism" without moving your lips. It may sound more like "then tillo klisen." That's it! That's how you do it. When you come to a tricky consonant, you use one that sounds a bit like it.
Practice the following: For bottle say gottle or dottle, for Mummy say nunny, for pepper say tetter or kekker.

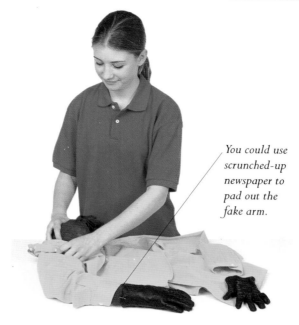

You could use scrunched-up newspaper to pad out the fake arm.

★ FALSE ARM DUMMY

Performing with a false arm attached to a box adds to the illusion that your dummy is alive. You could work out an act with a friend so there are three "people" in the show.

1 Stuff a stocking and push it into the sleeve of a large shirt. Pin a stuffed glove to the cuff to complete the fake arm.

2 The ventriloquist is helped into the shirt, pushing one arm into the empty sleeve, and keeping the other free.

Choose a sturdy box, big enough to completely hide your arm.

The audience can see your two "arms," and the puppet will look as if it is moving by itself.

Any glove or sock puppet works well in this act.

3 Put a glove on your hand in the shirt sleeve and a puppet on your free hand. Decorate a box and cut a hole in the back large enough to fit your arm through.

4 Push your hand with the puppet through the hole in the box, so it pops out of the top. Hold the fake hand with your real gloved hand, and the illusion is complete.

5 Get someone to interview you and the puppet. The puppet could start off friendly, become ruder and more uncontrollable, and even end up by attacking the interviewer.

"I'm a bit near-sighted. I can't see a thing. Let's try these."

"Hey! They're mine. I need them."

"It's okay. I'll do the looking, you do the talking."

"I don't know what to say."

"I do! Hi, kids! Good to see you. Let's do a show."

MIME

MIME IS ACTING WITHOUT SPEAKING. Instead of using words to tell a story, you use your face and body. Some mime artists paint their faces to exaggerate their mouths and eyes so they are more expressive. You can do a solo mime show, or include your friends in a mime troupe.

Mime makeup

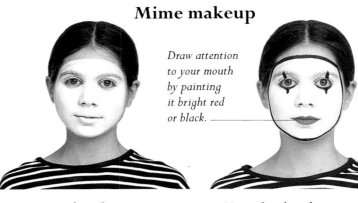

Draw attention to your mouth by painting it bright red or black.

1 Sponge white face paint over your entire face so it looks like a mask, ending at your hair and jaw line.

2 Use a fine brush to paint in the details around your eyes and lips. Now draw a thin black line to outline your whole face.

★ EXPRESSIONS

You can tell a whole story with facial expressions alone. Practice different expressions in front of a mirror. Imitate these expressions, then try others, such as scared, worried, sleepy, or proud.

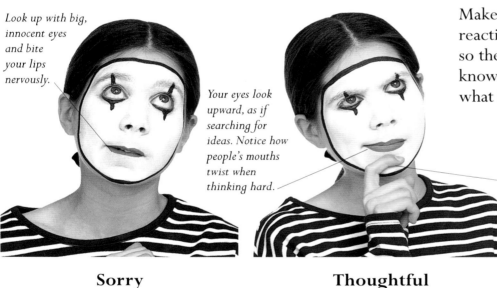

Look up with big, innocent eyes and bite your lips nervously.

Your eyes look upward, as if searching for ideas. Notice how people's mouths twist when thinking hard.

The finger on your chin helps the "thoughtful" look.

Sorry

Thoughtful

Pull down the corners of your mouth and raise your eyebrows. Tilt your head and look upward.

Narrow your eyes to slits. Stick out your lower jaw and make your mouth into a tight rectangle, as if you were saying "Grrrr."

Miserable

Furious

★ USING YOUR BODY

You can tell more complicated stories using your body as well as your face. Try stories such as "The Annoying Fly" or "The Sticky Chewing Gum." Make your actions and reactions really clear so the audience knows exactly what is going on.

The striped top is a traditional mime "look," but you can wear what you like — perhaps all black or baggy white, or a clown suit.

A famous director once said, "A clown must be able to weep with his knees." This means that your whole body must be expressive.

★ GUESSING GAMES

Here is a way to use mime to perform a guessing game show similar to charades. Your partner enters, holding captions such as "Guess what sport?", "Guess who's winning?", "What's happening now?", and so on. You mime the action and the audience calls out their ideas. When they guess correctly, your partner gives them the thumbs-up sign. You could do sports, food, musical instruments — even animals.

Your thumb makes a V-shape for the cue to slide along.

Keep your hands in line on the club, and fix your eyes on the ball.

Your muscles should bulge from the strain of pulling back the bow.

Make the audience see and believe in the ball as your foot makes contact. Follow the ball with your eyes.

Golf **Pool** **Archery** **Football**

Remember how ice cream melts? Lick it all round.

Only a mime artist can eat a huge hamburger without making a mess. Or can she?

Your flat hand helps the audience to "see" the saucer.

Let your fingers show how hard it can be to use chopsticks.

Ice cream cone **Hamburger** **Cup of tea** **Rice with chopsticks**

★ MIME WITH PROPS

In mime, you and the audience are using your imagination, so an everyday object, such as a short length of rope, can become anything you like. Think of as many uses for a rope as you can, then try with other objects, such as a hoop, a stick, or a sponge.

Explore the jungle in a dugout canoe. Keep an eye out for crocodiles.

Look down with your eyes open wide. Keep your arms up — and wobble!

The rope becomes a dangerous, hissing snake. Open your eyes and mouth wide in a silent, terrified scream.

Pull your whole body back and away from the snake or leap out of the way.

Canoe **Tightrope** **Snake**

MASK PARADE

THERE IS SOMETHING ALMOST MAGICAL about wearing a mask. It seems to change you completely, and people treat you differently, too. Masks are good for telling and acting out stories or for putting on a parade or pageant.

★ YOUR FACE AS A MASK

You can mask parts of your face with shadows by holding a lit flashlight under your chin. This is the perfect mask for telling really scary ghost stories in a darkened room.

A simple animal face design painted on a cutout cardboard shape makes an effective mask.

Try to find clothes with animal print patterns, or bits of fake fur, to add to the overall effect.

Dressing all in black will make the mask stand out.

★ PAPER BAG MASK

Place a large paper bag over your head. Put your fingers where your eyes are and get someone to mark the places with a felt-tip pen. Take the bag off BEFORE cutting out small eye holes using scissors. Cut out paper ears and hair and stick them on the bag, then decorate.

★ HALF MASK

Look in magazines for a picture of a big face looking straight ahead. Cut out the face, as shown, and stick it on cardboard. Make tiny eye holes and attach strings to either side of the mask. You could do a show where famous people step out of a giant television set and address the audience.

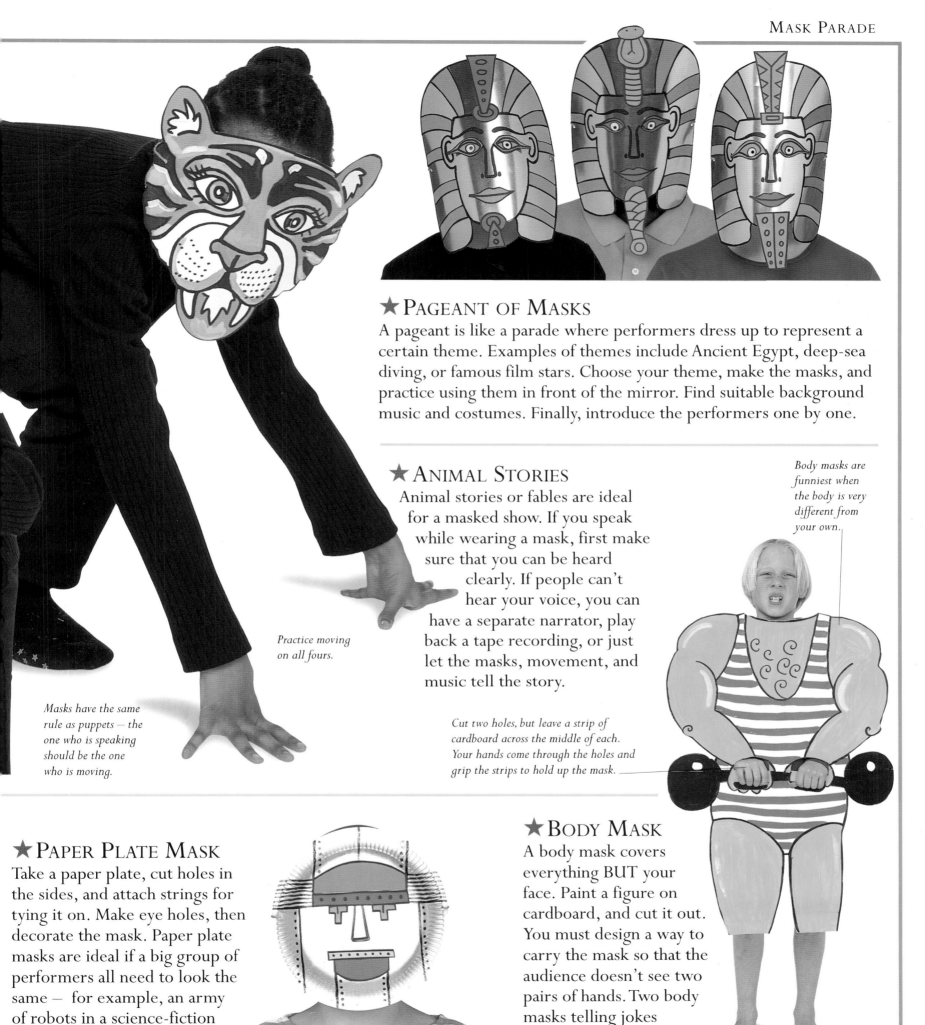

★ PAGEANT OF MASKS

A pageant is like a parade where performers dress up to represent a certain theme. Examples of themes include Ancient Egypt, deep-sea diving, or famous film stars. Choose your theme, make the masks, and practice using them in front of the mirror. Find suitable background music and costumes. Finally, introduce the performers one by one.

★ ANIMAL STORIES

Animal stories or fables are ideal for a masked show. If you speak while wearing a mask, first make sure that you can be heard clearly. If people can't hear your voice, you can have a separate narrator, play back a tape recording, or just let the masks, movement, and music tell the story.

Practice moving on all fours.

Masks have the same rule as puppets — the one who is speaking should be the one who is moving.

Body masks are funniest when the body is very different from your own.

Cut two holes, but leave a strip of cardboard across the middle of each. Your hands come through the holes and grip the strips to hold up the mask.

★ PAPER PLATE MASK

Take a paper plate, cut holes in the sides, and attach strings for tying it on. Make eye holes, then decorate the mask. Paper plate masks are ideal if a big group of performers all need to look the same — for example, an army of robots in a science-fiction adventure or a flock of sheep in a fable.

★ BODY MASK

A body mask covers everything BUT your face. Paint a figure on cardboard, and cut it out. You must design a way to carry the mask so that the audience doesn't see two pairs of hands. Two body masks telling jokes sideways to each other can be hilarious.

STAGE MAKEUP

With GOOD STAGE MAKEUP you can create really convincing characters. Try to copy some of these faces, using the basic techniques and special effects outlined below. Once you've got the face, you can put on a show.

BASIC TECHNIQUES

It is best to use water-based makeup or face paints. You can use cheaper makeup for details, but if you are sponging a layer of color over your whole face, you should get good-quality "pancake" makeup, which comes in a flat, round container.

Put gel and powder on the hair to blend in with the rest of the statue.

Remember to paint the neck and shoulders, too, if they are going to show.

Use a draped white sheet for a stone statue costume. You could paint "cracks" on it to make it look more realistic.

1 Start with a clean face. Test the face paint first on a small area to make sure you are not allergic to it.

2 Apply a base paint with a damp sponge, using long careful strokes. Blend in a second color.

3 Use different colors and a fine brush to paint in details, such as whiskers and lips.

★ HUMAN STATUE

Put on a wax museum show with living statues. Pose the "statues" on pedestals around a room. They should keep very still, although if you want to scare someone, a statue could suddenly "come to life."

★ TIGER

Enter on all fours, with the slinky movement of a cat. Your trainer gives orders, but you do the opposite. In frustration, she asks you to hold a hoop, while she shows you what to do. You stand up and applaud when she jumps through the hoop.

★ PIRATE

Pirates are fierce and adventurous. You could do a pirate show full of exploring, kidnapping, and swashbuckling action, using the stage combat on page 41.

★ CHINESE OPERA SINGER

Traditional Chinese operas have complicated plots about princesses, bandits, emperors, and animals. Create your own opera, and include dancing to Chinese music and kung fu movie-style stunts.

★ FROG

"The Frog Prince" is a famous story by the Brothers Grimm. You could turn it into a play or make up an ecology show about a frog that wants to preserve its pond.

SPECIAL EFFECTS

You can use special makeup wax to create bumps, wrinkles, and warts. Cereal flakes make good scabs, and raspberry jam is convincing blood.

Looking old

It is easy to add 70 years to your face with makeup. But don't forget to change the way you walk and talk, too.

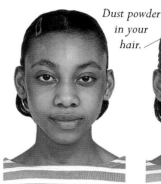
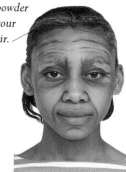

Dust powder in your hair.

1 Look in the mirror to see where the natural lines appear on your face.

2 Draw dark lines along these lines. Highlight either side with lighter paint.

Warts and scabs

If you are a warty witch or the victim of a mysterious plague, you will need some help from the makeup department.

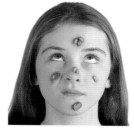

1 Stick cereal flakes or puffs on to your face with small pieces of wax.

2 Paint the flakes to suit the face. Add a touch of red for an oozing sore.

Gash

Need to look like an accident victim? Special-effects wax and fake blood come to the rescue!

1 Smooth a lump of wax onto your face with water.

2 Make a well in the middle and fill with fake blood.

★ CLOWN

There are some good clown ideas on page 25, but if you want to make up your own routines, remember that it's easy if you have a "straight" partner such as a Ringleader, schoolteacher, or parent.

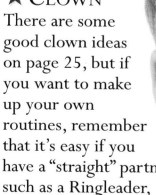

A clown face can be really colorful and decorative. This one has glitter gel on it to give it sparkle.

Paint a big, colorful smile, much bigger than your real mouth.

ILLUSION COSTUMES

LOOK AT THESE PICTURES. Aren't the illusions clever? Your audience is sure to be amazed and completely bewildered by them. But they are not difficult to make – all you need for most of them are some old clothes and a little imagination.

★ THE LITTLE WRESTLERS

You will need two hooded tracksuits in different colors. Push a pair of stuffed tights into the sleeves of both jackets. Pin stuffed gloves onto the cuffs for hands. Put inflated balloons into the hoods as heads. Lay the jackets on the ground and pin the arms around the "opponents' heads." Now get someone to help you put on the costume as shown.

★ THE EMU RIDER

Cut holes in the top and bottom of a large box and add legs, neck, head, and reins as shown. Climb into the box, and you are ready to ride. Practice so that the emu (the neck, head, and YOUR legs) has a mind of its own. Ride it! Talk nicely to it. Train it to step over obstacles and balance on one leg. Persuade it to kneel down and get up again, and hang on when it stampedes!

Put a small pair of shoes on your hands, pointing downward.

Pull a pair of running pants over your head, with a hole cut in the front so you can see and breathe.

Pin the jackets around your middle so the "heads" and "arms" are on your back.

Wear one pair of running pants normally.

Wear a pair of your own sneakers on your feet.

This costume transforms you into two wrestlers when you bend over and "walk" on both your hands and feet.

These are your real feet.

These "feet" are really your hands.

Make rigid reins from a wire coathanger so you can control the emu's head.

Use a light ball or a papier-mâché-covered balloon for a head.

Stuff the leg of a stocking to make the neck. Cut a hole in the box, and push the rest of the stocking through and fasten with tape.

Attach wide ribbons that will go over your shoulders to keep the box on.

The fight

You're ready for the Big Fight. Get a referee to give you a buildup, then come in on all fours, already fighting. The fight ends when the referee shouts "Break," and you can't. Slowly stand up to reveal your secret.

Keep your back moving to give life to the little fighters.

Stuff another stocking and place over the box. Put shoes on the end as feet, and attach them to the sides of the box in the position shown.

Wear tights that match the emu's neck so that your legs look as if they are part of the bird.

Do lots of kicking, tripping, pushing, and pulling.

Make a tail using strips of soft colored paper.

A pair of flippers make very funny bird feet.

20

★ BIG TUMMY FACE

Get someone to paint a face on your tummy and chest. Wear a jacket around your waist, and pull a sweater over your head. This costume is ideal for an Irish-style tap dancing show where only the legs move.

Pull on the sweater, but don't cover your chest. Instead, lift your arms up as if you were taking off the sweater. Now your face is covered and Big Tummy Face has a woolly hat.

Tie a scarf round the "neck" to hold up the jacket.

Tuck the sleeves of the jacket into the pockets, or pin on hands made from stuffed gloves.

★ THE GIANT

Take a piece of fabric 6 ½ ft (2 m) square. Fold in half, and sew along the side and top. Cut small holes for your arms and a bigger one for your head. Put on the costume and get a strong partner to lift you onto his or her shoulders. Now you can be a giant in a play or be interviewed as "The World's Tallest Kid." This becomes really funny if your stomach starts answering questions, too.

1 Stand with legs apart, wearing the costume and holding it tucked up above your waist. Your partner crouches behind you.

2 Your partner puts his head between your legs and carefully lifts you, keeping his back vertical – to avoid strain. Hold your legs firmly behind his back, and drop the costume over him.

Use thin, dark fabric to make the sack so your partner can see through it.

21

JUGGLING

HERE IS A WAY TO AMAZE YOUR FAMILY and friends. Juggling three balls with two hands is easy when you know the method. Once you have mastered basic juggling, you can try the following show ideas or learn some other skills that go well in a juggling show.

How to make juggling balls

1 Gather ½ cup (80 g) dry rice into a mound on a double square of plastic wrap. Pull up the corners to make a neat package.

2 Use a pair of scissors to cut off the neck of a round balloon. You will need three balloons for each juggling ball.

3 Stretch open one of the balloons and pull it over your rice package. Then pull the second and third balloons over the package.

Repeat Steps 1 to 3 to make three balls of equal weight and size.

LEARN TO JUGGLE

It will take you 20 minutes to learn to juggle if you spend five minutes on each of these simple exercises.

Focus on the balls when they reach the top.

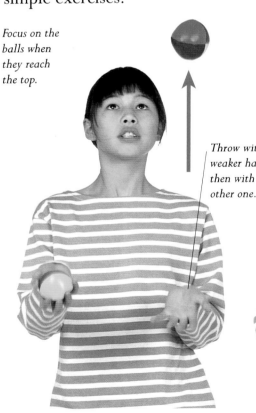

Throw with your weaker hand first, then with the other one.

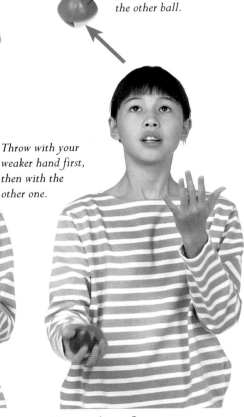

As this ball peaks, throw the other ball.

Try to throw the balls to roughly the same height.

Exercise one
Hold a ball in each hand and throw them both up at once, slightly higher than your head. Practice until you ALWAYS do good throws and good catches.

Exercise two
Imagine two bells in the air above your hands. Throw the balls up to make a "ding, dong, catch, catch" rhythm. Later, do "dong, ding, catch, catch."

Exercise three
Toss the balls, one by one, diagonally across your chest. The rhythm is "criss, cross, catch, catch." Now you're ready for real juggling – the three-ball cascade.

Exercise four
"Criss-cross" starting with your left hand. As the second ball peaks, make a third toss from your left hand, then the fourth from your right, and so on . . .

Juggling with one hand is easy. Just throw one ball straight up and throw the second when the first one peaks.

You must carry each scarf up and across your body. It is hard work!

★ JUGGLE LUNCH

Use two balls and an apple. Occasionally juggle two balls in one hand while taking a bite of the apple. It looks funny if you bite the wrong one.

★ JUGGLE SCARVES

Juggling scarves lets you juggle in slow motion. Use large, light, nylon scarves or soft plastic bags that drift through the air.

★ DIABOLO

This ancient Chinese toy spins rapidly on a string. Use one hand to pull on the string and make the diabolo spin. Experts can throw and catch it, and do lots of other tricks.

If the diabolo tilts, the control (pulling) string can push or pull it level again.

You won't be able to hold two big balls in one hand, so get a friend to throw in the first flying ball.

★ FLOWER STICK

Use a stick in each hand to gently toss the Flower Stick from side to side in midair. It looks magical.

Catch and "lift" the Flower Stick just above its center point. Don't hit it hard.

Throw your ball high in front of your partner's farthest shoulder.

★ HUGGLING

Huggling is easy. You and a friend each become one arm of a very wide person, then juggle normally.

Scoop the ball upward with a big open hand.

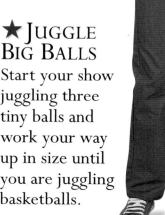

★ JUGGLE BIG BALLS

Start your show juggling three tiny balls and work your way up in size until you are juggling basketballs.

CLOWN SHOW

CLOWNS DON'T ONLY APPEAR in the circus. They turn up at festivals or parties and even on the streets. Putting on your own clown show could not be easier – just choose a clown character and make up funny routines, using these silly gags.

THREE BASIC CLOWNS

There are three main types of clown – Funny, Sad, and White-faced. With these three you can make anything funny.

OTHER CLOWNS

Clowns come in all shapes and sizes. Try making these special costumes for long-legged and tubby clowns.

A party wig and a big red nose finish off this outfit.

Make a giant bow tie, and borrow a tiny jacket.

Find an old jacket to cut up into rags.

Make a ruff from white fabric gathered onto elastic.

You can sew a sequin design onto a plain vest, or you might find a ready-to-wear sparkly one.

This all-in-one suit has a hoop sewn into the waist.

Wear battered, outsize boots.

Wear pale tights and stylish, shiny shoes.

Funny Clown
Funny Clown has NO dress sense – the clothes don't fit and clash horribly. But Funny always looks on the bright side, and finds everything absolutely hilarious.

Sad Clown
Ragged, unshaven, and miserable, Sad Clown is always in the wrong place at the wrong time. Funny bosses him around, and White-faced ignores him.

White-faced Clown
White-faced Clown is very elegant. He or she usually gives all the orders and doesn't laugh much. The act gets funny when the other clowns make mistakes and White-faced gets angry.

Tubby Clown
Find, or ask someone to make, a pair of trousers with a very wide waist. Then sew a hoop into the top.

Long-legged Clown
Follow the directions for making and wearing a giant costume on page 21, but use bright, patterned fabric to get a clownish look.

★ CLOWN ACTS

The best clown acts or gags are very simple. Their success lies in how you perform them. Use lots of rude noises and exaggerated gestures.

The gargle

This is a classic three-clown gag. To prepare, Clown One holds a glass of water and Clowns Two and Three have some water in their mouths.

Remember, a little water can have a big effect.

Clown One takes a sip of water.

Clown Two gargles loudly.

Clown Three spits it out.

Sad Clown looks embarrassed, as if Funny Clown has pulled off his pants!

The string of hankies

When another clown pulls a hanky from your pocket, it is tied onto another hanky, and another, and finally, out come your spotted undies!

The big weep

When you take out a hanky to cry, hide a wet sponge in your hand. Then you can wring out the sopping wet hanky to show just how sad you are and how many tears you have shed.

Hold the hanky so that it hides the sponge from the audience.

A stream of "tears" pours out of the hanky.

Open out the hanky before you sneeze so the bits of paper can fly out.

The big sneeze

Stuff a hanky with pieces of torn-up tissue paper, confetti, or talcum powder. Then sneeze loudly, blowing hard into the hanky. Make sure you do this leaning right over a member of the audience or another clown. This is a particularly good gag to try out on White-faced Clown, who will get really annoyed.

25

CIRCUS

THE NICE THING ABOUT putting on a circus is that everyone can be a star! You can all do the things you are really good at. You will be introduced as "The World's Greatest...," and you should perform as if you really ARE the greatest.

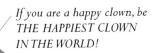

When you want the audience to clap, play the FLOURISH – a drum roll followed by a cymbal clash.

Circus band
A circus band can be lots of children playing funny instruments or just one drummer who plays along with all the action.

★ THE SHOW
You should have lots of different acts with plenty of variety. Some acts can be daring, some funny, some colorful, and some plain stupid! Rehearse so that the show goes smoothly, with the clowns filling the gaps between acts.

If you are a happy clown, be THE HAPPIEST CLOWN IN THE WORLD!

The Ringleader
The Ringleader makes a grand entrance, striding into the ring and announcing: "Ladies and gentlemen, boys and girls. Welcome to the Best Show in the World – THE AMAZING CHILDREN'S CIRCUS!"

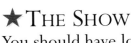

The Ringleader is usually dressed in a stylish jacket, black or white trousers, tall boots, and a top hat.

The ring
You can make a circus ring with cardboard boxes. Arrange the audience around the ring so lots of people will be in the front row.

★ CLOWNS
The clowns are always full of mischief, and often get chased around the ring by the Ringleader. But remember, you are really acting, and you should rehearse your gags.

★ THE SPINNERS

This show could include Hoop Spinners, Baton Twirlers, Ribbon Twirlers, and Rope Skippers. Start with just one performer, and build up until the ring is full of movement.

A circus secret — big hoops are easier to use than small ones.

★ CIRCUS ANIMALS

Dress up as animals and practice movements and sounds. You could be scary big cats or a herd of emus with brave riders (see page 20).

Animals can wear masks (see page 17) or makeup (see page 18).

In a Human Pyramid, a small acrobat (the Top-mounter) stands on a STRONG part of the others (the Understanders).

The Spotter is there to make sure no one gets hurt. But she can still smile and have fun.

★ THE ACROBATS

Get a soft mat or mattress and do an acrobatic display. Include forward and backward rolls, cartwheels, splits, handstands, or any other moves you can do well and safely.

The Understander makes sure the Top-mounter never falls.

Perform each movement as neatly and precisely as you can — keep your legs and back straight, and point your toes.

27

DANCE

YOU DON'T HAVE TO be a great ballerina to put on a fantastic dance show. There are plenty of fun shortcuts, but you will still need to practice hard and learn some steps.

Dance Hints

Check the floor where you are going to perform. Mats may make you trip or slide. A hard wooden floor is ideal for tap dancing. **If you are using** CDs or cassettes for music, you may need someone to be your sound engineer and play the right tracks when someone signals, or "gives the cue."

A dance show is a spectacle, so make sure your costume, hair, and makeup are all perfect.

★ TAP DANCING

Real tap dancers wear special shoes with metal taps. They train for hours each week to get their legs and feet to move incredibly fast. You could try this make-believe tap dance by having a friend offstage playing a fast rhythm with spoons on a tray.

Bang the tray really hard, so the "taps" can be heard clearly over the dance music.

Keep your face and arms relaxed, while your feet move at top speed.

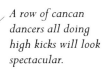

A row of cancan dancers all doing high kicks will look spectacular.

★ CANCAN

The cancan is an athletic, high-kicking dance. Try this trick to become an exciting cancan dancer. Your partner, wearing shorts, lies on her back. You sit across her tummy, facing her toes. You should wear a full skirt that covers her knees as she moves her legs to perform the cancan.

★ BALLET

If you have learned the five basic positions and some of the moves of classical ballet, you should listen to some music you love, and make up, or "choreograph," a dance that tells a story. A favorite is "The Dying Swan" to music by Saint-Saëns.

Gather several layers of stiff net onto a waistband to make a simple tutu.

The leader should use only moves you have all rehearsed.

★ JIVING

Jiving is a very energetic rock and roll dance from the 1950s. Do it with a partner. Hold hands and swing around, twist under one another's arms, and shake your hips in time to the beat.

In competition dancing, the gentleman usually wears a number on his back.

Wear a wide skirt that will flare out as you spin around.

★ SHADOW DANCING

This is one dance show that will look good without too much practice. One dancer stands in front, and the others copy her moves. If she doesn't change too quickly, it can look really slick.

★ BALLROOM DANCING

Social dancing is fun, but for a show you should learn the steps of the waltz, cha-cha, and tango. Then make it flashy, with swirls, dips, and arm movements.

Occasionally shout "Yee Haw!"

To get the country look, wear a checked shirt, vest, blue jeans, and boots.

A classic move called "scootin'" is done by lifting your left knee and hopping forward on your right foot.

Tuck your thumbs in your belt and look serious.

★ LINE DANCING

Line dancing can work in much the same way as shadow dancing. Wear cowboy and cowgirl clothes and put on some country music. Stand side by side in a line behind the leader, and copy the leader for each verse. Then make a right-angle turn and follow a new leader.

ROCK CONCERT

Y OU DON'T NEED TO PLAY an electric guitar or own a drum set to stage a rock concert. Just decide how many are in the group, choose a style of music you all like, make some fake instruments, dress the part, and you are ready to rock! But be warned – you are going to be making a lot of noise, so get an adult's permission first.

Sound

Your first step is to listen to CDs and cassettes and choose the songs you are going to play. It is a good idea to have a sound engineer, who tapes all the songs in order and makes sure the music runs smoothly during the concert.

Paint a tennis ball silver, and stick it onto the end of a toilet paper roll to make a convincing microphone.

Paint big cardboard boxes to make speakers. Stack them in huge piles around the stage.

A light show really adds to the atmosphere.

Cut out a guitar shape from thick cardboard, and paint it to look real.

Lights

With an adult's help, try the following effects: sweeping spotlights made by strong flashlights, lights flashing in time to the beat, or a bright backlight, shining from behind the band.

30

AD ACHE

★ HEAVY METAL CONCERT

Get the heavy metal look with long, loose hair (or a wig) to whirl and thrash around, a vest or baggy black T-shirt, fake tattoos on shoulders and chests, tight trousers or jeans with chains hanging off them, and crazy makeup with dark lips and weird, jagged shapes. Remember how you've seen real rock stars perform on television or videos and try to move like them as you mime along to the music.

Make a banner from paper or an old sheet and put the band's name on it in big letters.

Cover an ironing board with paper to make a keyboard. Stick on even lengths of wide black tape for keys.

Make a drum set from painted cardboard boxes and upside-down pails.

Gel your hair into spikes and spray it wild colors.

★ PUNK

Wear torn T-shirts with lots of safety pins and chains. Do plenty of leaping and screaming.

Wear huge, scruffy boots with no laces.

Wear a cap back to front on your head.

★ HIP HOP

Look the part in a big, puffy jacket and baggy shorts. Watch music videos to get ideas for some really cool moves.

Frizz your hair with a curling iron or by making lots of tiny braids when your hair is damp.

★ DISCO

Use plenty of glittery blue eyeshadow and wear shiny clothes. With some friends, work out a dance routine with lots of big arm movements to perform in unison.

Wear flared trousers.

31

MAKING MUSIC

Most musical instruments are based on plucking, scraping, banging, and blowing. Why not invent your own instruments and form a band to play them? You could start by using some of these musical inventions.

SIMPLE WAYS OF MAKING MUSIC

You can buy plastic or metal kazoos, but this is the do-it-yourself version.

Comb and paper
Fold a piece of tissue paper across a comb. Put it against your lips and hum a tune. It will sound quite different, and much louder.

Like the reed of a saxophone, the grass vibrates as you blow on it. The sound bounces off the inside of your cupped hands.

Blade of grass

Thumb sax
Hold a wide, strong blade of grass as shown, and blow between your thumbs. It will make a crazy screech, but you can change the tone by making the "echo chamber" of your cupped hands bigger or smaller.

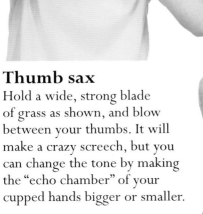

Wrench-o-phone
Borrow a selection of metal wrenches and tie them together with strong string, small to big, as shown. Tie them to a wooden rod at the top. Bang on the wrenches with a metal spoon or another wrench.

Make a rippling sound by running another wrench up and down the string of wrenches, or strike each one separately to play different "notes."

Play your drums by hitting the ends of the pipes with your hands.

Pipe drums
Get a long plastic pipe, 4 in (10 cm) in diameter, and ask an adult to cut it into four different lengths. Bind the pipes in a row, as shown, with foam tucked in between to keep them apart. Stretch balloons, with the necks cut off, over the top of the pipes, and secure with elastic bands.

★ THE BAND

Get together with some musical friends. You will need a conductor whose job it is to signal when to start playing and when to stop. A good conductor also controls the band's tempo (rhythm and speed) and volume. You could play and sing well-known songs, play along to a CD or tape, or do the sound effects for a dance or mime show.

★ THE RECITAL

If you are learning to play a musical instrument, it is a good idea to practice giving a recital. It is always nice if people throw flowers at the end, so drop some hints. A recital can be a song, a story, or a poem.

Jingle pole

Ask an adult to nail lots of metal bottle tops, two on each nail, into a strong stick. The bottle tops should rattle on the nails when you bang the stick on the ground.

Big bottle shaker

Put two large spoonfuls of dried beans or rice into an empty plastic soda bottle. Push a stick into the top and secure with tape.

Wear your best clothes and perhaps a flower.

Have an assistant turn the pages.

Use a music stand for a professional touch.

Decorate your bottles with paint.

The jingle pole and the shakers are the band's rhythm section.

There are three techniques for playing shakers — shake, rattle, and roll!

The bottle tops must be loose enough to rattle.

Beat the base of the stick on the ground in time with the music.

Try your microphone first to find its best position. Stand away from your speaker to avoid "feedback" (howling noise).

★ SING YOUR FAVORITE SONG

Everyone can sing and an audience always loves a song – especially if it is one they know. Little children can sing nursery rhymes, but you can sing anything. Karaoke soundtracks provide music for you to sing along to. If you are really brave you could sing without any accompaniment.

FASHION SHOW

PUTTING ON A FASHION SHOW is easy — you don't have to learn words, you hardly have to act — and people love watching you. You can use this style of show to present all kinds of themes.

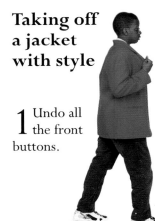

1 Undo all the front buttons.

2 Slip the jacket back over your shoulders.

RUNNING A FASHION SHOW
You will need models, clothes, and a place to parade. You will also need an announcer who will introduce "The Collection." The announcer can read from a script, but should be ready to improvise if there are any delays.

Use face paints to create special skin effects for some of your stranger costumes.

Your bizarre alien outfits can have extra limbs, heads, and eyes.

★ THE HISTORY OF FASHION
"Ug, the caveman, is wearing a beautiful over-the-shoulder leopard skin dress." Start with "Cave-wear Classics" and work your way right through to present-day fashions.

Try to really get into your character — he has not eaten for a week.

★ TODDLER FASHION
"This delightfully dotted two-piece ensemble is perfect for the junior sun-seeker." Assemble a group of toddlers (with their parents' permission, of course), and let them choose their own outfits, or dress them in adults' clothes.

They are cute when they get it right, and even better when they get it wrong!

★ ALIEN FASHIONS
"Green is THE trendy color on Mars this year, and this ensemble is ideal for long-eared monsters." Create the weirdest alien outfits you can imagine.

3 Slip your hands inside the sleeves, and let the jacket glide down your arms.

4 Catch the jacket with a hand on each side of the collar.

5 Hold the center of the collar in one hand, and swing the jacket over one shoulder.

How to turn like a model

1 Try to maintain good posture as you turn. Put your right foot just in front of your left, pointing slightly to the left.

2 Rise up onto the balls of both feet and about face.

Keep your back straight and head held high.

3 Lead with your right foot back down the catwalk.

★ HAUTE COUTURE
"Our lovely bride is a vision in foil and plastic." Top fashion designers create some extraordinary clothes. You can do the same, using foil, bubble wrap, even old bedsheets. Look in fashion magazines for inspiration.

Fashion models just ooze self-confidence.

Haute couture, or high fashion, shows traditionally end with a wedding dress.

★ FAVORITE FASHIONS
"These cycling shorts give you lots of freedom of movement." You can choose fashionable, useful, or silly combinations of clothes from your own closet for this show. With your parents' permission, you could also raid their closet for a show called "Clothes of Yesteryear."

You don't have to stick to walking up and down the catwalk. Depending on what you are modeling, you can leap in the air, dance, or even turn cartwheels.

Use tape or staples to hold your creation together.

The catwalk
If your show is at school or in a shopping center, you may have a real catwalk — a long, low platform with a T-shaped end and a screen covering the entrance to the dressing room. If you are at home, you should still mark out a catwalk, but have the audience sitting on the floor so they look up at the models. Your costume changes could happen behind a screen or in another room.

VIDEO

WITH A VIDEO CAMERA, you can make a show to watch again and again. A professional film company uses thousands of dollars and lots of people to make even the smallest advertisement. But if you can use a camera, you can make a video for next to nothing.

Video Hints

When panning (slowly moving the camera around), stand with your feet in the FINAL position.
Don't zoom in too much. Zooming out often works better.
Avoid aiming into bright lights.
When everyone is ready for the first shot, the director says "ACTION" and the camera rolls. To end the shot, the director taps the cinematographer on the shoulder. If you shout "CUT," you will hear it in every scene!
Tapes are cheap. Always start with a new tape. Don't risk erasing your aunt's wedding!

★THE STORY

You can copy what you see on television, like a music video, a sports event, a news story, or an interview. Or you could write your own drama.

The assistant director carries the storyboard, makes notes, and watches continuity.

The cinematographer must know exactly what to shoot. Don't get in her way.

The "gopher" does everything else. ("Go for this, ... go for that, ... ")

The director directs rehearsals, checks everything, and says "Action."

CHARACTERS

You can manage with a few kids, a happy dog or cat, and maybe a helpful adult. If you need a pirate or a frog prince, see page 19 for ideas.

THE CREW

You will need a director, who may also be the writer, a cinematographer (camera operator), and an assistant or two to do everything else, such as carrying things, asking the public to keep quiet, and checking continuity.

You can film "intertitles" to explain things.

THE NEXT DAY...

LOCATION

The location is where you shoot the action. Avoid dark or noisy places. Keep the camera away from water and dust. Your backyard or local park would be ideal. Ask an adult if you need permission.

SOUND

Most video cameras have built-in sound. Test your camera first to make sure it is picking up your voices. On some cameras or VCRs you can record another track of music or sound effects later.

★ STORYBOARD

Draw a picture of each part of the story. Shoot the film in this order, otherwise you will need to edit the story together later, and that gets tricky. Rehearse it a few times, checking camera angles and making a note of the time needed for each shot.

Don't stick to long or middle-distance shots. Use close-ups for variety and to change the atmosphere.

The bullies won't let our heroes join in their football game.

Our heroes decide to go exploring in the forest instead.

The bullies decide to chase the heroes.

One bully trips and falls into a puddle, another tears her shirt on a thorny branch.

The bullies end up lost, cold, and miserable. The heroes watch from behind a bush.

The heroes make wolf howls and owl hoots to scare the bullies and teach them a lesson.

The heroes relent and pop out of the bushes and offer to help the bullies.

The heroes use their tracking skills to find a way out of the forest.

The next day they all go exploring together. The ball is left behind on the field.

CONTINUITY

You must remember from one shot to the next exactly what everything looked like. Your hero cannot wear shorts in one shot, and a split second later, be wearing jeans — unless your video is a story of magic, and anything can happen! Can you spot the continuity mistakes in these two pictures?

Picture one

Picture two

TITLES AND CREDITS

The titles (at the beginning) and credits (at the end) give details such as the name of the movie, who appeared in it, and who made it. You could film someone writing the details — on paper or maybe in sand — or you could try animation. This means mounting the camera on a tripod, then shooting a tiny bit at a time, gradually changing what the camera sees. You could use plastic letters that seem to un-jumble themselves to form the words you want.

Picture Two: Bottle is full; boy's cap is missing; blue beaker has been added; extra cake on plate; girl's headband is missing.

MAGIC SHOW

EVERYONE LOVES MAGIC. Some people love to be fooled and make a great audience. But BEWARE! Some don't. Watch out for this second type. You'll have to charm them with comedy. Always be polite to your audience.

★ A SHOW WITH AN ASSISTANT

You will need a jacket with lots of pockets to conceal your tricks, and an assistant who can be constantly amazed by your magic. Start with simple routines, then look in books and magic shops for more ideas. Here are a few to get you started.

His shirt is sloppy, but he can't understand why you are UNDOING the buttons at his neck and cuffs.

Give a good sharp tug – it looks impossible.

He trusts you completely. You are the magician.

Incredible shirt removal

Tidy up your scruffy assistant. Undo his shirt cuffs and top buttons. Stand behind him, grab his collar, and PULL the whole shirt right out of the jacket. He looks astonished – but he is really in on the secret. It all depends on your preparation.

★ CLOSE-UP MAGIC

If you are doing a show on your own, try tricks like these two that you can do "before their very eyes."

Magic corks

Challenge a volunteer to hold the corks as shown (to the left), and to swap hands using fingers and thumbs, without putting them down.

☞ Your secret

There is only one way to hold the corks. Practice this grip until it is easy.

☞Windows of fate

To prepare this trick, cut three strips of strong paper, about 6 ½ ft (2 m) long, and 3 in (8 cm) wide. Glue to form three big loops, BUT…

☞Your secret

The first has NO TWISTS in it.

The second has ONE TWIST in it.

The third has TWO TWISTS in it.

The routine

Ask three volunteers to choose a loop or "window of fate" and to step through it. Then you cut each loop in half, lengthwise. Amazingly, the first ends up as two big loops. You say: "You'll receive a new bicycle." The second turns into one huge loop. You say: "You'll travel around the world." The third ends up as two interlinked loops. You say: "You're in love with someone, but only you know who!"

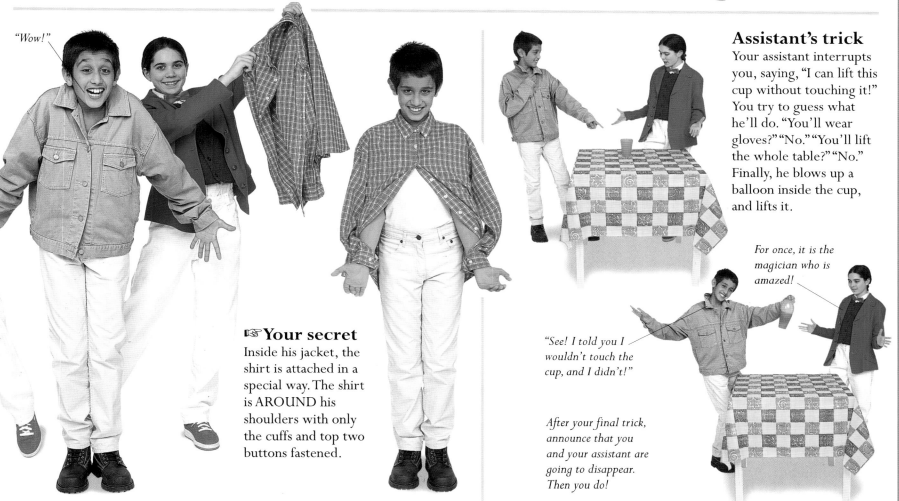

"Wow!"

☞Your secret

Inside his jacket, the shirt is attached in a special way. The shirt is AROUND his shoulders with only the cuffs and top two buttons fastened.

Assistant's trick

Your assistant interrupts you, saying, "I can lift this cup without touching it!" You try to guess what he'll do. "You'll wear gloves?" "No." "You'll lift the whole table?" "No." Finally, he blows up a balloon inside the cup, and lifts it.

For once, it is the magician who is amazed!

"See! I told you I wouldn't touch the cup, and I didn't!"

After your final trick, announce that you and your assistant are going to disappear. Then you do!

The jumping rubber band

Put a colored rubber band on your two big fingers. Say a magic word, blow on your hand, or sprinkle it with invisible magic dust. Close your fist for a moment, open it, and WOW! the band jumps across to your other two fingers.

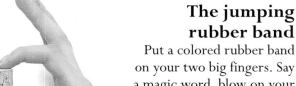

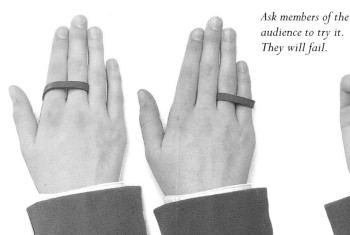

Ask members of the audience to try it. They will fail.

☞Your secret

When you make a fist, tuck all four of your finger tips under the rubber band. When you open your hand again, the band will appear to jump across.

PUTTING ON A PLAY

A PLAY IS A STORY BROUGHT TO LIFE. A "script" is a play that has been written down. There are several ways for you to find a script. Look in your local library or write a script of your own. You could adapt a story you have read or improvise a story with your fellow actors. Whatever you do, you will need time to learn lines and rehearse.

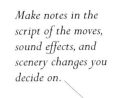

Make notes in the script of the moves, sound effects, and scenery changes you decide on.

★ AN IMPROVISED SCRIPT

As a group, think of some characters and a plot, then try out a scene, talk about it, and try it again until it feels right. When you are satisfied, write out the final version – the script. Make sure your play has a good beginning, an entertaining middle, and a great ending.

Rehearsals

The first step is to vote on who will be the director. The director's job is to decide how certain scenes should be played, keep the action moving along, and work out the actors' moves. Remember, actors do not always have to face the audience. They can turn away as long as they can still be heard.

★ PROMENADE THEATER

Here is a good idea if you are putting on a show at home for a small audience. As the scene changes, the audience follows the actors. This means you can change scenery in one place while the audience is in another. You can move from room to room inside, or perform outdoor scenes in the backyard.

A PRISON CELL (indoors). Scenery includes a barred window and a prison door.

A FOREST (in the backyard). A sign on a tree helps set the scene.

Scene One

"What's that?" asks the mysterious lady to distract the officer as she slips some keys to the wrongfully imprisoned prince.

Scenery

Scenery lets the audience know where the play is taking place. You can paint a large "backdrop" on cardboard or a sheet to hang behind the actors, or you can paint signs or smaller pictures and leave the rest to the audience's imagination.

Scenery does not have to be realistic. This window is used to represent a palace.

Don't panic if you forget your lines. Listen for the prompter, who will get you going again.

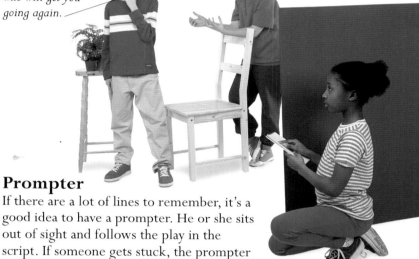

Prompter

If there are a lot of lines to remember, it's a good idea to have a prompter. He or she sits out of sight and follows the play in the script. If someone gets stuck, the prompter helps by whispering the next line.

★ STAGE COMBAT

If your play is an action-packed adventure such as a spy thriller or pirate tale, you may need to include some fight scenes. There are some golden rules for stage combat. Actors must never get hurt. The "victim" is in charge of every move. NEVER improvise a fight — carefully work out all the moves beforehand.

Pulling by the ear

You "cup" your hand around the victim's ear. He holds your wrist firmly with both hands and PUSHES. This looks as if you are pulling him!

The punch

You both stand sideways. The attacker punches the air between the victim's face and the audience. It is the victim's reaction that makes it look good. She stumbles backward holding her face.

The attacker slaps her thigh as she makes "contact," or someone offstage can clap at the right moment.

Scene Two

The prisoner prince flees, with the officer in hot pursuit. The officer hunts for tracks to help her find the prince.

THE ROYAL PALACE (back indoors). The stage crew has transformed the room with a throne, a portrait, and a window.

Scene Three

The mystery lady turns out to be a princess in disguise. She takes the prince to her father, the king, to receive his royal pardon.

PUBLICITY

IF YOUR SHOW is just for family or friends, you can simply invite them to come. But it is fun to do some publicity anyway, to make it all more special. If your show is for the public, then there are lots of ways to attract a crowd.

POSTERS

Get everyone in the group to create a poster. They can all be different, but NOT TOO DIFFERENT. So if you are putting on a gothic horror play, tell the artists they can use only black and blue and MUST include bats! Photocopy the details and stick them on the posters. With your parents' permission, go around your neighborhood and ask if you can put up posters in places such as stores, libraries, schools, and laundromats.

PRESS RELEASE

About two weeks before the show, send a letter to the editor of your local newspaper or the newsdesk of your local radio or television station. Include all the relevant information as shown below. The paper may want to come and photograph a rehearsal. Have everything ready, and if you have a good idea for a picture, suggest it, but then leave the decision to the photographer.

The Editor
The Echo
10 Main Street
Springfield

Dear Editor:

Where will it be performed?

What is the show (is it a play, a circus, or a concert)?

Announcing a performance of the gothic horror play, NIGHTMARE AT THE CASTLE.

Who is putting it on?

Place: Springfield School Auditorium

Date: Saturday, October 8, at 3:30 pm

When does it take place?

Performed by the Springfield Drama Group

How much will the tickets cost?

Admission $2.00

Tickets can be reserved by calling the school

How can tickets be reserved?

A benefit for Springfield Animal Shelter

Call 222-234-5678 for further information.

Why is it being put on (for example, if you are raising money for charity)?

Don't forget to give a contact telephone number for inquiries.

The director says: "We can promise you a SHOCKING evening's entertainment — a real ROLLER-GHOSTER RIDE!"

Add a personal quote.

NIGHTMARE AT THE CASTLE

SATURDAY OCTOBER 8 3:30 pm

Use bold lettering that will catch people's attention and can be read from a distance.

BANNER

The place where you are performing always looks better with a big banner outside. This should be drawn on paper first, then drawn to scale on cardboard or canvas. You could print a banner on a computer. It will look more appealing if you then paint and decorate it to make it look original.

NTS:

ASTLE

HOOL AUDITORIUM

AL SHELTER
INFORMATION

Enlarge a photograph on a color copier and stick it onto a big star.

LOBBY DISPLAY

Make a display of photographs of performers, rehearsals, or previous productions. You could include "Quotes from the Critics" like "Absolutely wonderful!" – Sarah's mom.

BOX OFFICE AND TICKETS

If you have a set number of seats, the house manager makes a diagram and writes the names on squares as tickets are bought and seats reserved. It is a good idea to leave a few seats unreserved, and some standing room for people who forget to plan ahead.

Explain how long the intermission will last and where and what refreshments will be sold.

Design individual programs, or get them photocopied.

NIGHTMARE
AT THE CASTLE

Act One
The dinner party

Act Two
A game of hide-and-seek

**Intermission
20 minutes**
Punch and cookies will be
served in the lobby.

Act Three
The corpse

Act Four
Whodunnit?

PROGRAM

You can either give or sell programs to the audience. The program should have a decorative cover, and inside, the following should appear: A Program of Events, including the intermission, words of any sing-along songs, a list of all the performers and crew, and thanks to the people who helped and lent you things.

BACKSTAGE CREW

IF YOU AND YOUR FRIENDS decide to put on a big show, you will need to do lots of planning beforehand so it goes smoothly and is a big success. Decide on a show that suits your talents — a play, a circus, or a variety show with lots of different acts. Of course, you will need performers, but there are also plenty of essential backstage jobs.

Mark the floor with crosses of colored tape, so you know exactly where to put things.

STAGE MANAGER
You and your assistants must set and move all props (objects actors need while on stage) and stage furniture at the right time. You don't have to do this in the dark, but do it efficiently, without attracting too much attention. The stage crew traditionally wears black during performances.

You'll find some great costume ideas among your parents' castoffs or in thrift shops.

DIRECTOR
You must make the decisions, but like the captain of a sports team, you help the team members stay happy and do their best. They must also make it easy for you to be the boss!

Make your instructions clear and keep a record of what you decide.

DESIGNER
If you are good at art, you may be given the job of designer. You should show the team your sketches for costumes, backdrops, props, posters, and so on. Once they agree on the designs you should make them — but get the crew to help.

Live sound effects can be fun.

You can use reading lamps or spotlights as footlights.

SOUND ENGINEER AND LIGHTING TECHNICIAN

The sound engineer records music and sound effects and plays them back at the right moment, at the right volume. You should have a technical rehearsal to get this perfect. The lighting technician plans, with an adult, the best way to light the show. You will give the cues (instructions) to the adult, who will operate the switches at the right time.

COUNTDOWN TO SHOWTIME

It's the big day and there are lots of last-minute things to be done. It may help to write out a checklist to make sure nothing is forgotten. Everyone has a special job to do.

🕐 Director: Have the company and crew arrive at least an hour before the show for makeup, costume, warm-up, and final directions.

🕐 House Manager: Set out seats and put up signs for the exit and restrooms. Make sure the box office staff is ready to sell tickets.

🕐 Sound Engineer: Set all cassettes and sound effects and do a sound test to make sure that the volume controls are set at the right level.

🕐 Performers: Stay calm and quiet in the dressing room. It is okay to be nervous, but never be selfish. Always consider and help the others in the show.

🕐 Lighting Technician: Make sure that the lights are all working and house lights are ready to go on.

🕐 Stage Manager: Set all props on a special prop table – not to be touched! Get the stage crew to set the stage for the first act and wait for the house manager to give you the cue for:

🕐 CURTAIN UP!

WARDROBE

The person in charge of the wardrobe organizes all the costumes and accessories and keeps them in order. Before the show, hang up the costumes on a rack, ready for quick changes.

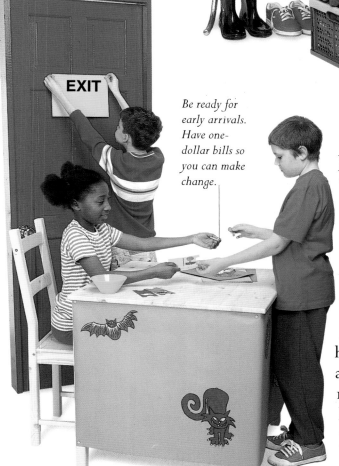

EXIT

Be ready for early arrivals. Have one-dollar bills so you can make change.

Make sure all the accessories for each costume are easy to find.

HOUSE MANAGER

Your job is to help the audience enjoy the show. You should organize the box office staff, who will sell tickets and allocate seats. You and the ushers will show the audience to their seats, make sure they have programs, and tell them about the intermission and refreshments. You might also like to arrange a surprise party for the cast and crew after the show.

SHOWTIME

T<small>HE LAST TICKET IS SOLD</small>, the audience is seated, and the final notes of the entrance music die away. The house lights dim, the stage lights shine, and it is "curtain up" and on with the show!

The ushers may start applauding to get the audience going.

THE EMCEE

The emcee (master of ceremonies) enters, warmly welcomes the audience, and introduces the acts, one by one. "Ladies and gentlemen, boys and girls, please welcome the magnificent, world-famous WHAM BAM BONGO BAND!"

"I can't wait to see the show."

★ THE VARIETY SHOW

A variety show is a performance with lots of different acts. Look through this book and choose four or five different things to do. The whole show should last less than an hour. You can combine acts, like a circus in mime, or a fashion parade in masks, or decide to link all the acts with one theme, like Halloween, A Day in Space, or Around the World.

Showtime Hints

Think carefully about the order of the program. The first act should be the one that needs the most setting up, and you need a good strong act to finish.
The house manager and ushers should prepare for the intermission rush, with drinks already poured and food ready.
When it's all over, return everything you have borrowed, clean up all the messes you have made, and give signed programs and a big "Thank you" to all the adults who have helped you.
Now start planning your next Showtime!

When the show is over the emcee invites the entire cast back on stage to take a bow. Your big smile and outstretched hands are a way of saying "Thank you" to the audience.

"That was the best show I've ever seen."

INDEX

Acknowledgments

Dorling Kindersley would like to thank the following people:
Michael Michaels and Elaine Elliott of the **Waltham Forest Youth Theatre** for their assistance in arranging for the following people to appear in the book: Alexandra Achille, Samantha, Serena, and Stephron Andrew, James and Janice Anjo, Geoffrey Benn, Miriam Billig, Ellen, Joseph, and Tessa Buddle, Sandra and Tom Campbell, James Gray, Katie Grundy, Ellie and Ravi Muniandy, Hazel Ocskò, Anna and Nicola Rawlings, Isaac Roberts, Anneli Stollar, Ana Tewson Bozic, Robyn Turp.

Additional design assistance: Tina Borg, Jacqui Burton, Jacqueline Gooden, Tory Gordon Harris,

Rebecca Johns, Chris Scollen
Additional editorial assistance: Gill Cooling, Amanda Rayner, Jane Yorke
DTP design: Nomazwe Madonko, Andrew O'Brien

Additional Models: Cassie Curran, Fred Kirby, Taskin and Tolga Kuyucuoglu, Natasha Trinnaman
Additional Photography: Steve Gorton, Ray Moller, Kim Sayer, Steven Wooster
Costumes: Barbara Owen
Face painting: Stephanie Spyrakis
Illustrations: Dorian Davies
Model making: Jim Copley
Production: Kate Oliver